Learning to Listen to Learn

Using multi-sensory teaching for effective listening

Helen White & Christina Evans

P·CP

Paul Chapman
Publishing

Lucky Duck is more than a publishing house and training agency. George Robinson and Barbara Maines founded the company in the 1980s when they worked together as a head and as a psychologist, developing innovative strategies to support challenging students.

They have an international reputation for their work on bullying, self-esteem, emotional literacy and many other subjects of interest to the world of education.

George and Barbara have set up a regular news-spot on the website at http://www.luckyduck.co.uk/newsAndEvents/viewNewsItems mand information about their training programmes can be found at www.insetdays.com

More details about Lucky Duck can be found at http://www.luckyduck.co.uk/

Visit the website for all our latest publications in our specialist topics

- Emotional Literacy
- Bullying
- Circle Time
- Asperger's Syndrome
- Self-esteem
- Positive Behaviour Management
- Anger Management
- Eating Disorders

ISBN: 1-4129-1157-5

Published by Lucky Duck
Paul Chapman Publishing
A SAGE Publications Company
1 Oliver's Yard
55 City Road
London EC1Y 1SP

SAGE Publications, Inc.
2455 Teller Road
Thousand Oaks, California 91320

SAGE Publications India Pvt Ltd
B-42, Panchsheel Enclave
Post Box 4109
New Delhi 110 017

www.luckyduck.co.uk

Commissioning Editor: George Robinson
Editorial Team: Mel Maines, Sarah Lynch, Wendy Ogden
Designer: Helen Weller

Printed in Great Britain by The Cromwell Press, Trowbridge, Wiltshire

Contents

How to use the CD-ROM

The CD-ROM contains PDF files, labelled 'Worksheets.pdf' which contain worksheets for each lesson in this resource. You will need Acrobat Reader version 3 or higher to view and print these resources.

The documents are set up to print to A4 but you can enlarge them to A3 by increasing the output percentage at the point of printing using the page set-up settings for your printer.

To photocopy the worksheets directly from this book, set your photocopier to enlarge by 125% and align the edge of the page to be copied against the leading edge of the copier glass (usually indicated by an arrow).

Preface

This programme is concerned with listening as auditory and visual attention, rather than listening as a comprehension activity. Effective listening may appear to be common sense, but in reality it is a complex activity, which benefits from direct teaching. Professionals need training in how to teach and engage in good listening behaviour. We have called the programme *Learning to Listen to Learn*, and it will lead to improvement in social skills and assist classroom management

We have a keen interest in helping students to find new ways to learn, with a particular interest in improving listening and thinking skills. In our professional lives we sometimes support pupils with impaired language development in mainstream classes at secondary school to help them access the language of the curriculum. During these support sessions we observed that increasingly teachers were repeating instructions three or more times, only to have pupils ask, 'What do we have to do?' We realised that the listening skills programme, which we had used with our pupils in the Speech and Language Centre for many years, would benefit all mainstream pupils as well.

We are fortunate in that the Speech and Language Centre is sited in a very forward thinking school, Lampton School in Hounslow, which is always seeking new ways to challenge pupils' learning. Lampton, despite having pupils speaking more than 50 different languages, is one of the highest rated schools for value added education. Susan John, the headteacher, believes strongly in keeping abreast or ahead of new ideas and it was her faith that allowed us to be able to develop a programme which could be used to train all mainstream pupils. Although the programme has been mainly written for secondary pupils, it can be adapted and used by primary pupils, business people and parents/carers.

We developed two sessions, one for listening 'to make friends' and one for listening 'to learn'. It was decided that we would train all the new Year 7 pupils at the beginning of the school year and so the programme commenced. Although neither of the authors had ever taught a class before we managed to hold each class's attention by the very nature of the skills they were learning. The programme has been running for six years which means that every pupil in the school has been trained in the active skills needed for listening, and it has become a school-wide policy to remind the pupils of these skills in every lesson, when the teacher is instructing the whole class. Other schools and other professionals showed a lot of interest as the programme became more widely known and we became involved in training adults in how to use it. Finally, when the Commissioner for London Schools, Professor Tim Brighouse, chanced upon a class we were teaching and requested a copy of the programme it was decided to publish.

Tim Brighouse wrote:

> I was being given a whistle stop tour of Lampton School when I glimpsed some magic. It was the authors of this book engaged with a Year 7 class in something that was so enthralling that they quite failed to notice my sudden appearance with the headteacher in the classroom.
>
> There was something else unusual – namely the presence at the back of the room of a dozen or so other adults who turned out to be fellow teachers.
>
> 'What's going on here?' I enquired in a whispered intrigued aside to the headteacher. And that's when I learned about 'Learning to Listen to Learn' and how it was a vital part of the Year 7 curriculum. The fellow teachers were attempting to make sure that they reinforced the skills that the Year 7 pupils were all learning, in their teaching of other subjects.
>
> Naturally I was impressed because it's always seemed to me that acquiring the habits of behaviour and the associated carefully practised skills are essential to everyone and there's probably no better time to focus on them than during the first year in secondary school, when sadly it's all too often the case that youngsters slip backwards in their learning and most importantly in their confidence.
>
> So 'learning to learn' courses become part of any school's repertoire of programmes for Year 7 – to be reinforced at regular intervals in later adolescence.
>
> Ever since my visit to Lampton School I've been telling other schools of their practice and I'm delighted that the outstanding practitioners involved have now written a book to make some of their knowledge and practice available to others.

Introduction and Rationale

For many years there has been a major focus in education on the content of the syllabus and its delivery. There has been far less interest in how students are receiving this information and their understanding and learning from it. In other words, listening and attending appear to be considered automatic reactions in children. In contrast to this there has been an increasing realisation in business that a good communicator, which inevitably means a good listener, is the person who will succeed and should be valued. Professional teams are often trained in how to listen actively to others.

Schools have traditionally focused on the teaching of language skills through reading, writing and spelling, speaking and listening. Although the first four are explicitly taught, there has been little attention paid to the fundamental skills needed for listening. Yet good listening underpins everything we do. Educators are paying increasing attention to it and it has been included as a separate part of the National Curriculum. However, in this context it usually refers to the process of comprehension of spoken language, as in, listen for and recall the main points of a talk, reading or television programme. (DfEE 2001). It is not seen as a set of active skills that need to be taught. When we deliver our programme to the pupils, each class group identifies at least thirteen different skills that produce optimum listening. It is accepted that listening involves attention, but how this is brought about has not been comprehensively addressed. Yet there are many children with very limited listening skills sitting in classrooms and not attending to the teacher's message. Some of them will also be disrupting the learning of other students who are attempting to learn but are prevented by noise or interruptions.

The importance of listening and language development to learning

Listening and attention are learnt behaviours. If one is born into a family where there is constant noise and people do not listen to one another, obviously one will not acquire the necessary skills. Research from the Basic Skills Agency in 2003 indicated the concern of headteachers that the behavioural and verbal skills of children starting school were at an all-time low. Many children were unable to sit still and settle in school, were unable to follow instructions and were not ready to learn.

Listening begins well before a baby is born. In fact it has been discovered that a foetus will move a specific muscle when it hears a specific speech sound (Tomatis 1991). Karass et al (2002) studied infant attention, mother's encouragement of her child's attention and how both factors work together to foster language development. They found that boys' language development depended on their level of attention and maternal verbal encouragement of attention. Shared attention with an adult, and good listening, are critical to early language development. When these are absent major difficulties ensue. Dr Sally Ward (1984) who was principal Speech and Language Therapist for Central Manchester Healthcare Trust over a period of ten years, searched for a connection between the oft-repeated complaint, 'Kids just don't seem to listen any more', and the growing numbers of children with delayed language development. Her findings, that one in five children is harmed simply by the fact that the TV, VCR or radio is constantly on, were frightening. Many parents leave the TV on all the time for company and to occupy their children. In addition, there are many other noisy machines at work in households these days such as washing machines, vacuum cleaners and dryers. The link between listening problems and household noise was established when Ward visited the homes of 373 children with delayed language development, picked up by health visitors who had used Ward's test on 1000 children in Manchester. For most of the sample of 101 babies with listening problems, their only quiet period alone with a parent was bath time and bedtime. For one in seven, even these occasions were filled with background noise. In the first crucial months of life, babies may have difficulties hearing their parents talk above the household noises, at the developmental stage when they need one-to-one interaction with other humans in order to distinguish between meaningful sounds – their parents' speech – and meaningless background noise. Ward's research (1984) found that one in five children had listening and attention problems and this incidence had doubled between 1984 and 1990. "For a lot, all the parents needed to do was turn off their telly, while for others they needed to do other things as well, such as talk to their children more or use 'motherese' (baby talk). A lot of middle-class adults, especially teachers, won't do it and talk to their infants as if they were 20. It causes all sorts of problems."

The problem also affects play – children in the control group played normally at the age of three while the experimental group did not. "There's a big problem with play and children now," said Ward. "Children are not playing normally and adults are not playing with them. You can sit a kid in front of a box of toys and he won't know what to do with them."

Another piece of research by Betty Hart and Todd R. Risley (1995) from America demonstrates that a key ingredient in determining future social class is language – the basic tool for thought, argument, reasoning and making sense of the world. Their research on young children's language is one of the most thorough studies ever conducted. Three groups of children from welfare, working class and professional families were tape-recorded throughout their first years. Researchers counted and then extrapolated all the words a child would hear and speak in every encounter with its parent or caregiver. When they analysed the hours of recordings, the sharp class differences in the three groups' early experiences were startling.

By the age of four, a professional's child will have had fifty million words addressed to it, a working-class child thirty million and a welfare child just twelve million. They found that the professional child at the age of three had a bigger vocabulary than the parent of the welfare child. The way children were spoken to was also measured – how much they were listened to, explained things, given choices and in what tone of voice. At the age of three the professional child has had 700,000 encouragements addressed to it and only 80,000 discouragements. But the welfare child will only ever have been encouraged 60,000 times in its life, suffering twice as many discouragements. When the children in the study were measured at aged nine to ten, Todd and Risley concluded: 'We were awestruck at how well our measures of accomplishments at three predicted language skill at nine to ten.' In other words, school had added little value after the age of three – it was already too late.

Research published by the government's Basic Skills Agency (2003) found head teachers believed that, compared with five years ago, fewer pupils now had basic language skills, such as listening and talking to others. There are many factors involved in this issue cited by researchers, including insufficient parent communication and excessive television viewing, particularly in small children. A large study by Christakis et al (2004) in the US found that for every hour of television watched daily, toddlers faced a ten per cent increased risk of attention problems. The neuropyschologist Jane Healey states (1991) that:

> A 'good' brain for learning develops strong and widespread neural highways that can quickly and efficiently assign different aspects of a task to the most efficient system... Such efficiency is developed only by active practice in thinking and learning which, in turn, builds increasingly strong connections. A growing suspicion among brain researchers is that excessive television viewing may affect the development of these kinds of connections. It may also induce habits of using the wrong systems for various types of learning.

As children develop these neural highways they also develop control and focus of higher-level cortical function: they develop an attention span.

Some educational practices may also be implicated in hindering children's spoken language development. A study by Locke and Ginsborg (2002) found that children's language skills did not necessarily improve once they were in school or nursery. The language development of 240 children aged three to five years from deprived areas was studied. Many children were lagging even further behind after up to two years of nursery and reception education, and some of the more able children actually seemed to have deteriorated in their language skills. The researchers attributed their findings to the children's limited exposure to spoken language at home and also to their subsequent early years education. They comment that a premature focus in the foundation years on literacy, at the expense of spoken language, has a deleterious effect on spoken language and therefore subsequent academic progress. Clearly many factors are affecting the lowered levels of attention, listening and spoken language seen in many classrooms today.

Attention and listening can be taught

Children and adolescents can develop the mature attention spans they need for effective thinking and problem-solving in today's complex world. These skills can be taught in school, just as they can be taught in the business world. If the individual can also understand why these skills are important and how they will improve their lives, both socially and academically, they will choose to adopt them. It is vitally important that the students should clearly see the implications for good listening behaviour, and that they understand why some individuals should choose to distract and disrupt others so their motivations are evident to all. In this way, positive change can be achieved. In recent years there has been a lot of concern expressed over people's inability to remain focused and to be aware that a teacher, colleague, parent or another adult is giving important information. This was particularly noticeable when important instructions were given at the beginning, but it also applied during the lesson when further instructions were given. The problem of how to ensure that the children were listening to the important initial information was becoming more urgent. These instructions set the ideas, concepts, the context and the links for the new information that is to be absorbed. It has also become evident that there is a high level of interruption, chatter, disruption and general hubbub that is difficult to eradicate.

In the wider world it means that we have become poorer at listening to one another. In the workplace this can lead to misunderstandings between colleagues, to mistakes being made and to poor performance. In the classroom it means that there is a loss of valuable learning time in an overcrowded curriculum.

Pupils who have a specific language impairment (SLI) are taught skills that others are able to automatically learn such as:

- how to filter out background noise or visual distraction
- to believe in themselves
- to believe that the task is possible
- to sit as close to the teacher as possible
- to face the teacher
- to have the best light on their work
- to establish a good relationship with the teacher.

But, as can be seen from research such as Ward (1984), Hart and Risley (1995) and Christakis (2004), non-SLI children are not automatically learning the aforementioned skills. We began to think that the skills taught to SLI children would benefit ALL children and the germs of the programme were born. We were fortunate in that we worked in a school where new ideas were allowed to flourish and the opportunity to put 'listening skills' into place across the whole school was accepted enthusiastically. The programme began by targeting all the new Year 7 pupils across the school. It was so enthusiastically received by the teaching staff, that it was incorporated into the school's programme as a permanent feature. The programme has been in place for six years and during that time has been refined to the current model.

Children already spend enormous amounts of time in schools and don't lack opportunities to practise listening. What they do need is specific instruction on how to listen. Targeting listening skills is one of the ways to help them understand the cues and signals that a teacher uses when she wants to focus their attention. As teachers become more informed about the listening process, they will have the tools to adapt their teaching styles to the needs of a variety of students. Not only will it benefit children with attention deficit disorders, learning disabilities, hearing impairments, speech and language difficulties, emotional difficulties and those who speak English as a second language, but it will benefit all other children as well.

The Structure of the Programme

This programme comprises a short series of interesting lessons and games to teach people how to listen and attend. It covers both active listening in conversation and effective listening and attention in large groups. There are clear and detailed lesson plans, activities, questionnaires and posters. There are follow-up activities to ensure long-term improvement in listening skills. The purpose of this programme is to encourage participants to formulate their own ideas, which can be translated into skills that they can use throughout their lives, and particularly to be able to use them in other learning situations. It encourages respect for others, shows them how to maximise the listening process and helps with self-awareness. The programme has already been successfully used in a number of secondary and primary schools over a period of five years. The feedback from the teachers involved has been 100% positive.

> "It's great. It really works." Richmond, Surrey Secondary teacher.

> "It's a whole-school approach to good listening skills." Middlesex Primary teacher.

> "I'm delighted to come to a new school and find this in place." Hounslow Secondary teacher.

> "Provides good classroom control in order for learning to happen." Isleworth Primary.

> "Excellent – made me understand what it must be like for some pupils during lessons." Chiswick teacher.

The programme has been designed so that teachers and trainers can assess its advantages quickly and understand how it enhances learning and control in the classroom. It fits easily into the curriculum because it does not take up much time. Teachers are able to see the difference immediately. Pupils, who are encouraged from the outset to generate the ideas, are able to see that it helps them to concentrate and to remain focused. They are taught the reasons behind the different strategies so that they immediately want to use them. They learn that good listening skills help to foster good social skills and tolerance. Because the programme helps people listen to each other's point of view it has benefits in Pupil Referral Units and in families as well as the classroom.

It helps the pupils who do not know how to listen and reduces the time that the teacher must repeat instructions. How often do we hear, "What are we to do Miss?" after the teacher has given instruction several times?

Who should use this programme?

The programme is designed for use with mainstream students in Key Stage 2, 3 and 4 and can be adapted for adults. It can also be used for students with special needs.

Teachers, teaching assistants, speech and language therapists and trainers can lead the sessions.

What will the programme achieve?

It will improve the level of attention and listening in the classroom. It increases the effectiveness of the teacher in transmitting information to students and consequently the level of learning taking place in a lesson. A simple way of examining this process is as follows: There are essentially two aspects of attention: visual attention (looking at a subject) and auditory attention (listening to a subject). Information is input into the brain through looking and listening and held in the working memory. Previous knowledge about this topic is activated from the long-term memory store and understanding of the information then takes place.

Why attention is essential for understanding

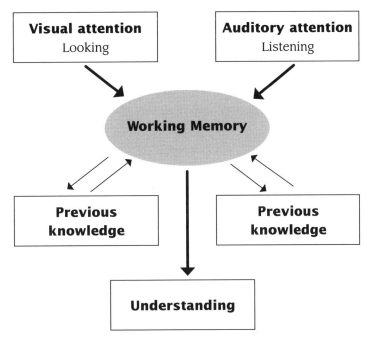

Through the *Learning to Listen to Learn* programme students have more awareness of the complex processes involved in listening and can therefore take a more active role in creating a listening classroom. Class control becomes simpler. The role of the listener in conversation is also developed, encouraging more effective communication and socialisation.

How was the material developed?

On the occasions we were supporting speech and language impaired children in the classroom we often observed the frustration of staff that were teaching well-planned lessons. Although some of the students were ready and alert, there were frequently a number of pupils who had not listened to clearly given instructions. The teacher had to repeat the information more than once, wasting class time and disrupting the flow of the lesson. We discussed how this behaviour could best be dealt with, comparing it to the listening of our students from the Speech and Language Centre who have been specifically taught to listen.

It was decided to take the techniques that speech and language therapists and teachers use to improve attention and listening, and develop them for use with mainstream classes of Year 7 pupils. We were astonished at the interest of the mainstream pupils and staff in understanding the process of listening and how quickly they adopted the techniques we explained to them. The total and complete attention of up to 30 individuals in a classroom on a speaker created an almost tangible energy in the room. The stillness in the room and the absorption of the listening students allowed the teacher to speak quietly but magnified the power of the words.

The success of the programme meant that it was used with subsequent Year 7 pupils as they entered the school. Staff enthusiasm led to requests that the programme be adapted for use with Key Stage 4 students and for use with other schools in the area. This book will give teaching staff the background knowledge and skills to increase the attention and listening behaviour of their pupils.

How to Use the Programme

There are three sessions. The first two sessions are given a week apart and the third is a booster session.

Teaching Methodology

Although the operation of this programme can be carried out in any situation, companies and schools particularly, for the purposes of this book the programme is designed around the classroom situation. Although the programme is written mainly for Key Stage 3 it can easily be adapted and used for Key Stage 2, Key Stage 4 and adults. We have given training at both primary and secondary schools and found that they were able to use the same methodology and materials, by adjusting their language level at which they delivered the sessions. Nearly all the materials are suitable for all ages, in fact some of the secondary students will enjoy the games with noises as much as the primary. Trainers will select appropriate materials for their audience from the range provided in this book.

Timing

The listening programme is designed to be taught over two 50-minute sessions. This can take place at the beginning of the school year for Year 3, Year 7 or Year 10 pupils starting a new Key Stage in their school career. There should also be a review session six weeks later and further review sessions annually. In order that all the teachers in the school understand the rationale and benefits, they should undergo training beforehand in the methods so that they are aware of the many skills required in the action of listening. Active listening then becomes a whole-school issue and is adopted as a learning tool for every lesson. Additionally it is a very useful tool for classroom management. Pupils will benefit from the consistency throughout all aspects of school.

Groupings

The students work in whole class groups of up to 30 at the beginning of the first session for the initial modelling and analysing part of the programme. Approximately 20 minutes into the first session they are asked to work in pairs with the person they are seated alongside to practise the skills they have identified. Each pair is nominated A or B by the teachers at the stage that practice is needed. The whole group resumes during the review at the end of the first session.

During the second session, the whole group remains together throughout, except in the short activity phase when they may work in pairs.

Rooming

In some schools, particularly in London where they are situated near busy roads or under the Heathrow flight path for example, the ability to hear the teacher is problematic without taking into account any disturbance within the class. We found vast differences in the classroom environments according to the building and/or the classroom where each session took place. In general, older classrooms were smaller, less ventilated and less soundproofed, the pupils were more crammed together and thus the pupils were more distractible or more listless. Science laboratories were not ideal because of the uncomfortable stools and because there were sockets or taps to fiddle with. Similarly, the Technology rooms were not ideal because they had noisy machinery to contend with as well as tools to fiddle with. On the other hand, when the sessions were held in the school's new building, where the temperature, noise and space have been optimally designed, the environment was ideal for listening and the pupils were more contented and attentive. It is important therefore, to be aware of the environment in which the pupils are learning and to assess whether they are good enough for the pupils to hear instructions.

Seating

We found the way that pupils were seated in some classrooms to be such a problem that it was decided to treat it as a separate issue.

In many classrooms listening is a problem because some of the students are seated with their backs to the teacher (it is very difficult to listen to someone with your back turned to them – try it!) or turned sideways to such an extent that it is uncomfortable to turn their heads to face the teacher for any length of time. As a result these students are deprived of the opportunity to use many of the skills listed later in this book. These pupils are the ones who can often be seen fiddling, chatting or otherwise disturbing others. The move to group seating became the norm in the seventies following the Plowden Report (1967). Galton et al (1999) comment that:

> It would appear that two decades of classroom research, curriculum reform on an unprecedented scale and a shift in educational thinking which has called for a return to whole class teaching and more subject specialism has had almost no impact on the way teachers organise pupils.

For effective listening the students should all be seated so that they are directly facing the teacher and this position should only be altered if they are doing small group work.

A recent study by Hastings and Chantry Wood at Nottingham Trent University (2000) has concluded that the practice of seating pupils in groups, although potentially useful, is inflexible and cannot be justified as standard practice by observations of what actually takes place in classrooms. They comment on the body of robust and consistent research evidence collected over the last twenty years concerning the effects on children's attention and distraction when seated in normal groups and in other configurations to work on their individual tasks. Hastings and Chantry Wood cite evidence from studies that found significant differences (16–124% longer on task) when comparing the impact of group seating on pupils' attention with that of other arrangements, typically pairs facing the same direction. There are two important effects. Firstly, almost all pupils' attention to their individual work increases when they sit in pairs, or in arrangements in which no one sits opposite them, as compared with group seating. Average gains of more than 30 percent are common. Secondly, the pupils who benefit most are those who are the most distracted when sitting in a group. Many double their time 'on-task'. When undertaking individual work in rows, the variation between the most and the least attentive almost disappears; in group seating arrangements, the range is substantial. The researchers conclude that the best strategy for teachers to adopt is to re-arrange seating as appropriate for the task being undertaken. This rules out group seating as the standard arrangement. Studies of teacher/pupil interactions and activities in primary school classrooms have shown that groups generally account for only 10-20% of teachers' interactions with pupils, of which, typically, just over one-third are 'task-focused' and can be construed as 'small group teaching'. In addition, most of this collaborative interaction took place between pairs of children, not within groups.

Resources
All the resources are given in this book, with the teaching programme. The ideas are generated by the pupils and written on the board as a list for them to use and remember. The skills are reviewed at the end of and the beginning of each session.

Photocopiable worksheets and posters are included; these can be printed from the CD-ROM included with this book.

Session 1
Social Listening

Introduction for Trainers Before Session 1 – Social Listening

Listening During Conversation

When two people are in conversation, it often seems that it is the speaker who is doing most of the work. To many people it appears that listening is a simple, passive activity: one that requires little effort in conversation. However, in recent years there has been increasing realisation that true listening and understanding of what one hears requires effort, focus and concentration. All too often when one partner in the conversation is speaking the other is not listening at all, but is thinking of his or her own point of view. They may be waiting, even longing, for the speaker to stop so that they can have an opportunity to articulate their thoughts.

A good listener is highly valued as a friend, a student and as a work colleague because we know that they have heard the message we want to convey – communication has been effective. It is vital to listen attentively in order to learn new information, avoid misunderstandings, solve problems, empathise and negotiate successfully.

The *Learning to Listen to Learn* programme teaches active listening in order that:

- One's own style of communication can be understood – awareness of strengths and weaknesses in listening are vital to help positive change.

- One can be an active listener – listen with a purpose and avoid your attention drifting.

- Non-verbal communication can be understood – increasing conscious understanding of the importance of non-verbal behaviours improves communication.

- Feedback can be given to help the speaker convey their message. This means growing awareness in the use of methods to help clarify the message the speaker is giving to avoid misunderstanding.

Learning Framework

The *Learning to Listen to Learn* Programme uses the framework of Model – Analysis – Practice to facilitate learning. Two adults are needed to model an activity. The students then analyse what they have watched and are invited to practise the skills for themselves. The active participation of the students ensures real engagement in the learning process.

Model 1

In Session 1 the adults model a conversation where 'bad' listening takes place:

Adult A introduces a topic they wish to talk about, such as something they did over the weekend.

Adult B looks away, fiddles with his or her watch, walks away to examine an item in the room, yawns, interrupts with a completely different topic, looks bored and generally shows complete disinterest in the speaker.

Meanwhile Adult A is valiantly battling on and trying to maintain the conversation.

Eventually A gives up and makes their farewell to B.

Analysis 1

Adult A asks the observers whether they think A would like B as a friend. When the resounding 'No!' is given, Adult A asks, 'Why not?' This leads into the analysis of the scenario they have just witnessed. This scenario introduces humour into the session that immediately engages the observers. It is also much easier for the students to analyse what is happening and spot the negative behaviours in the listening process. The students will now be able to identify the first 11 active listening skills from the list below.

Active listening skills

1. Eye contact.

2. No fidgeting.

3. No interrupting.

4. Staying on the subject – not interrupting with a different topic.

5. Facing the speaker.

6. Standing still.

7. Standing a suitable distance away, not too close and not too far.

8. Good body language – an alert posture expressing interest.

9. Interested facial expression.

10. No yawning.

11. Asking/answering questions.

The three remaining skills below might need to be elicited after the students have observed the adults model good listening behaviour:

12. Nodding.

13. Small words such as 'Mmmm' 'Really!' 'Oh no!' that let the speaker know you are actively involved in the conversation.

14. Mirroring – the subconscious way we copy each other's body language that increases rapport.

These listening skills can be printed out and used as a checklist for trainers.

The trainers stress how good listening skills help the speaker to continue because of the positive feedback they receive. It is possible for someone to listen without showing any of these behaviours (though it will be harder) but it is very difficult for the speaker to continue if they feel what they are saying is not being heard or valued.

Model 2
The adults have a second attempt at a conversation and this time B demonstrates excellent listening behaviour including the skills of nodding, small words and mirroring that the students will probably not yet have identified.

Analysis 2
As the students recognise the additional listening skills they are discussed. To illustrate the importance of nodding to maintain a conversation the trainer can relate this to television journalists and interviewers. The interviewers can be seen nodding strongly because they are inhibited from adding verbal feedback (small words) as this may interfere with the viewers' enjoyment.

Students are often unaware of the significance of mirroring the body language of one's conversational partner in establishing rapport.

Practice
The students now have an opportunity to practise some of the skills they have identified and to experience how it feels to be ignored and to be listened to carefully.

Session 1 – Social Listening

Conversational Listening to Make Friends

The first session is fundamental in helping the pupils understand for themselves the enormous importance of listening in:

- effective communication in relationships
- helping the speaker to continue
- making the speaker feel valued
- making friendships
- maintaining friendships.

Preparation

Trainers and teachers need to be familiar with the Learning Framework of Model – Analysis – Practice which is given in more detail in the Learning Framework on p17.

Classroom layout
All participants must be facing the teachers/trainers. Desks must be completely cleared.

Session Begins

Introduction
Participants are given a brief introduction, explaining the programme and its purpose. Two posters are put up as visual aids identifying the purpose of listening in each session, one saying, 'Listening to Make Friends, and the other saying 'Listening to Learn'. The students are then told that the adults will be having a conversation and that while they observe they should be noting any good/bad behaviours.

Listening task / modelling poor listening

Two adults model bad listening for three to four minutes while the whole group watches. This means that one of the adults starts a conversation and the listening adult displays all sorts of behaviours which disrupt the conversation e.g. changes the subject, disrupts, fiddles, avoids eye contact, turns away (refer to the Introduction for Trainers for Session 1). This part of the session will require practice by the adults to perfect because it is psychologically difficult for the speaker to maintain the conversation in this situation.

Analysis of poor listening behaviour

Students are then asked to identify and analyse what went wrong during the conversation they were listening to. Ask the questions:

'What were the problems with that conversation?'

'Would you want to be her/his friend?'

As the students offer their ideas, note them on the board as positive behaviours. For example, the pupils will say, 'She interrupted you' so the skill will be written up as 'No interrupting'. Then ask the question:

'Who has the more difficult/challenging role, the speaker or the listener?'

The pupils will by now identify that the listener has the more difficult part.

Listening task – modelling good listening

Adults model good listening. The listener will try to take on board the advice offered by the class. The speaker talks again and the listener demonstrates perfect listening.

Analysis of good listening behaviour

Pupils are again asked to analyse the conversation. Ask the questions:

'Was that better?'

'Would I want to be his/her friend now?'

Go through the skills written on the board and ask if there were additional behaviours shown that are not written up yet. The additional behaviours that become obvious from the good listening model are: nodding; little words such as 'Mmm', 'Yes', 'Oh dear'; mirroring body language/physical rapport.

Practice of bad listening to experience negative emotions

Pupils then practise bad listening in pairs. Each pair is given a label of A or B and each has a turn at speaking while the other exhibits bad listening behaviours, so that they can experience the negative emotions at being ignored.

Analysis of feelings

In the whole group once again, the adults ask the pupils:

'How does it feel when you aren't being listened to?'

Note responses on the board in a list.

Practice of good listening skills

Pupils now practise good listening in the same pairs. The adults circulate to comment upon the particular behaviours the pupils are demonstrating, such as mirroring, nodding and so on.

Analysis of feelings

Back in the whole group, the adults ask the pupils:

'How does it feel this time?'

The responses are noted on the board in a list alongside the other one.

The class is asked to look at each list to identify any common traits and then to compare the lists to identify what emotions are being shown. One list contains only negative emotions and the other list contains positive emotions. This leads to the revelation that good listening is very important in establishing and maintaining friendships.

Activities

The Key Stage 3 and older students are asked to complete the Skills Required for Good Listening worksheet, in which they identify a skill that they can improve. Key Stage 2 students can complete the worksheet, I Am A Good Listener.

If there is time, the session can be finished with any of the activities listed for Session 1.

Homework

Students are asked to look at their families to see who listens well and who listens badly. These observations are to be shared at the next session with humour and discussion will be about the impact on the individual.

Resources for Session 1 – Social Listening

A selection of games and worksheets are included for reinforcement and self-assessment of the students' listening skills.

Top Listeners

This game increases the students' awareness of the rules they are learning and provides practice in an enjoyable and fairly natural context.

Materials

- Top Listeners topic sheets – photocopy or print them out (preferably onto card) and cut into individual sections. Place a few of the cards into envelopes.

- Good Listener checklist.

- One-way Communication sheets.

- Two-way Communication sheets.

- Skills Required for Good Listening.

- I Am a Good Listener.

Rules of the game

- The teacher divides the class or group into groups of three.

    One student is the **speaker**.

    One student is the **listener**.

    One student is the **observer**.

- When given a signal the speaker selects a topic from the envelope and talks to the listener for a couple of minutes about it. The observer ticks the checklist as she/he sees the listener showing the target behaviours.

- The observer feeds back observations about:

    What you did well…

    What you could do better…

- The speaker feeds back how it felt to be listened to during that turn.

- Students change roles at the teacher's discretion.

- The teacher walks around the groups giving advice as necessary.

Listening Backwards – One-way Communication

An enjoyable game to demonstrate the importance of eye contact, gesture and asking questions in communication.

- Divide the group into pairs and label each individual A or B.

- Each pair sits back to back. Try to arrange the pairs so that they cannot see each other's pictures or they will have an advantage.

- A is given a picture and B has a pencil and paper.

- A's task is to describe the picture so that B, who cannot see it, can draw it fairly accurately.

- In 'One-way Communication' B is not allowed to ask questions. This makes the task very difficult indeed.

- When the pairs are ready they can compare their drawings to the original.

- Discuss what made the communication difficult:

  not being able to see their partner

  not being able to hear properly with the amount of noise in the room

  being unable to ask for clarification

  not being able to use gesture.

Listening Backwards – Two-way Communication

Now the game is repeated but this time B is allowed to ask questions.

- Again allow the pairs to compare their efforts when they are ready.

- Discuss what made the communication easier this time – being able to ask questions helped B to be more confident of what he/she needed to do.

Listening To

Make Friends

Listening To Learn

Active Listening Skills

1.   Eye contact.

2.   No fidgeting.

3.   No interrupting.

4.   Staying on the subject – not interrupting with a different topic.

5.   Facing the speaker.

6.   Standing still.

7.   Standing a suitable distance away, not too close and not too far.

8.   Good body language – an alert posture expressing interest.

9.   Interested facial expression.

10. No yawning.

11. Asking/answering questions.

12. Nodding.

13. Small words such as 'Mmmm' 'Really!' 'Oh no!' that let the speaker know you are actively involved in the conversation.

14. Mirroring – the subconscious way we copy each other's body language that increases rapport.

Top Listeners

What I like on TV	Dogs
Smoking	My worst meals
My family	Football
My favourite teacher	Spiders
Homework	If I won the lottery
Holidays	When I am grown up

Top Listeners

My favourite music CD	My favourite game CD-ROM
My favourite DVD	The best day I can remember
The place I like best	School uniform
The best story I can remember	My best meal
Friends	School trip
My favourite sport	My favourite lesson

Good Listener Checklist

How did the listener do?

	Excellent	Ok	Could do better
Looked at speaker	☐	☐	☐
Didn't fidget	☐	☐	☐
Nodded	☐	☐	☐
Didn't interrupt	☐	☐	☐
Asked questions	☐	☐	☐
Looked interested	☐	☐	☐
Good body language	☐	☐	☐

Best skill was:

_____

Skill that needs more practice is:

_____

Other comments:

_____

_____

_____

One-way Communication

1. Sit back to back with your partner.
2. Don't let your partner see your picture.
3. Describe your picture.
4. Do not answer any questions.

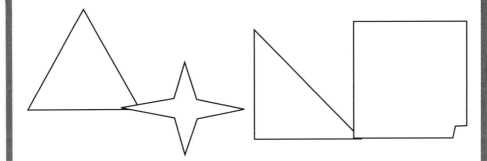

One-way Communication

1. Sit back to back with your partner.
2. Don't let your partner see your picture.
3. Describe your picture to your partner.
4. Do not answer any questions.

One-way Communication

1. Sit back to back with your partner.
2. Don't let your partner see your picture.
3. Describe your picture.
4. Do not answer any questions.

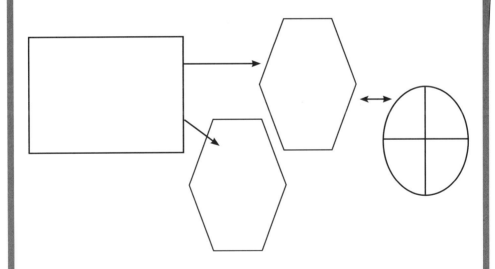

One-way Communication

1. Sit back to back with your partner.
2. Don't let your partner see your picture.
3. Describe your picture.
4. Do not answer any questions.

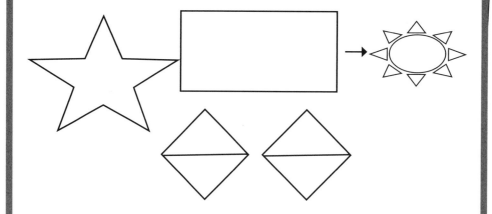

One-way Communication

1. Sit back to back with your partner.

2. Don't let your partner see your picture.

3. Describe your picture.

4. Do not answer any questions.

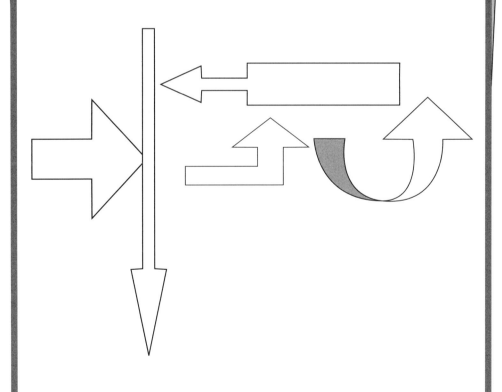

One-way Communication

1. Sit back to back with your partner.
2. Don't let your partner see your picture.
3. Describe your picture.
4. Do not answer any questions.

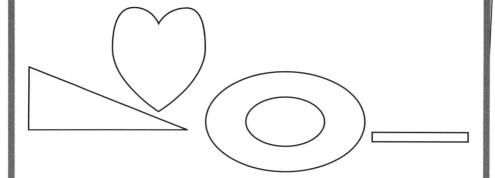

Two-way Communication

1. Sit back to back with your partner.
2. Don't let your partner see your picture.
3. Describe your picture.
4. You can repeat your instructions.
5. You can answer questions.

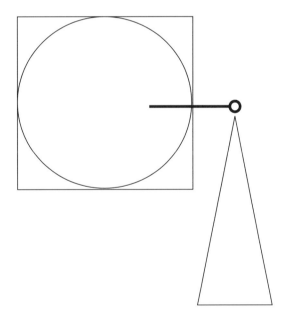

Two-way Communication

1. Sit back to back with your partner.
2. Don't let your partner see your picture.
3. Describe your picture.
4. You can repeat your instructions.
5. You can answer questions.

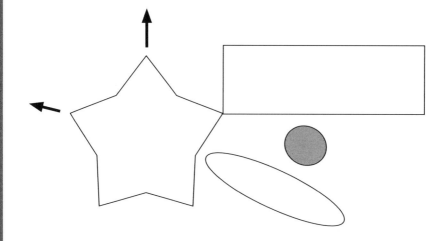

Two-way Communication

1. Sit back to back with your partner.
2. Don't let your partner see your picture.
3. Describe your picture.
4. You can repeat your instructions.
5. You can answer questions.

Two-way Communication

1. Sit back to back with your partner.
2. Don't let your partner see your picture.
3. Describe your picture.
4. You can repeat your instructions.
5. You can answer questions.

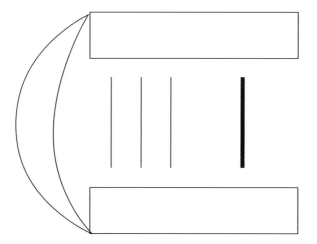

Two-way Communication

1. Sit back to back with your partner.
2. Don't let your partner see your picture.
3. Describe your picture.
4. You can repeat your instructions.
5. You can answer questions.

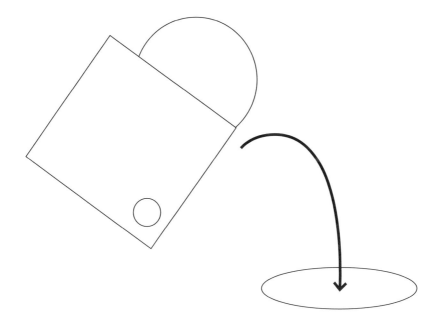

Two-way Communication

1. Sit back to back with your partner.
2. Don't let your partner see your picture.
3. Describe your picture.
4. You can repeat your instructions.
5. You can answer questions.

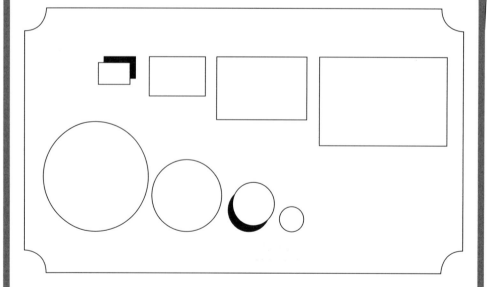

Skills Required for Good Listening

Name _____ Form _____

List the skills needed for active listening

_____

_____

_____

_____

_____

_____

_____

_____

The listening skill that I am best at is

_____

_____

_____

_____

The skill I would like to improve is

_____

_____

_____

_____

I Am a Good Listener

My name is _____

Draw a green circle round the things you are good at.

Draw a red circle around things you could do better.

I can...

Look at the person who is speaking

Take turns

Smile

Nod my head

Sit still

Not fidget

Not fiddle

Not call out

Ask questions

Always listen to my teacher

Think about what the person is saying

Session 2
Listening in the
Classroom

Introduction for Trainers before Session 2 – Listening in the Classroom

There are three main aims to this session:

1. Increase the students' awareness of the problems that can arise to hinder listening and learning in a classroom.

2. Demonstrate the sitting position to improve attention.

3. Allow the students to experience the transformation that can occur in their listening and retention through simple changes in the class behaviour.

Learning Framework

The framework of Model – Analysis – Practice is used again to improve the students' learning.

The basis of the first part of this session is to demonstrate a range of negative behaviours that frequently occur during a lesson that cause distraction and possibly disrupt the teaching and learning in the classroom.

Model
Adult B sits amongst the students who are asked to listen to the Martian Spacewagon passage read to them by Adult A. While this is being read Adult B sabotages the reading by exhibiting a string of disruptive behaviour e.g. tapping a pen, dropping equipment, searching through a bag, calling out, asking irrelevant questions, talking to a neighbour, asking the teacher (Adult A) to sort out who has taken her rubber, yawning loudly and rocking on a chair.

Analysis
These behaviours are discussed to show the negative effect they have on the rest of the class. The underlying emotional and/or learning problems the 'disrupter' may have are also highlighted.

Practice
The whole class practises listening at the end of the session with a very high degree of attention. Many students will comment on how completely different

this experience was and that it transformed their usual way of attending. They feel immersed in what they are hearing and are able to retain the information without effort.

The Sitting Position

We have found it useful to explain to the students, in a simplified way, what is happening in their brains when we teach them the 'sitting position' so that they understand the reason for adopting it. This is useful because the neurological evidence gives credence to the position and the students are practising the position without being aware of it while they listen to the explanation.

What is happening in the brain?

We are continuously bombarded with stimuli through our senses. All information entering our brains is received through our senses. The brain is sorting out and interpreting these sensations constantly. When we think about our senses, most of the time we only consider the five senses that take in information from outside our bodies: sight, touch, smell, taste and hearing. However, just as important to our lives is the integration of sensory input, which gives us information about gravity and motion and about our body's muscular movements and position in space – the vestibular system and proprioception. These play an important role in our awareness and our ability to understand and learn.

The vestibular system

This system maintains the orientation of the body, mainly the head, in relation to gravity when you are standing still and also in response to sudden movements such as acceleration, deceleration and rotation when you are in motion, as when walking (Tortora & Anagnostakos, 1990). The vestibular nuclei carries impulses from the semicircular canals and cerebellum to the Reticular Activation System (RAS) in the brain stem. The RAS is a nerve reticulum that carries impulses to the neocortex. Beginning in utero, the RAS increases responsiveness to incoming sensory stimuli from the environment. This gets us ready to take in and respond to our environment and to learn (Hernandez-Peon, 1969). This connection between the vestibular system and neocortex as well as the eyes and core muscles is highly important to the learning process. When we don't activate the vestibular system, we are not taking in information from the environment.

Proprioception

All of our muscles have proprioceptive receptors, which sense the degree of stretch in the muscle. These stretch receptors let us constantly know everything about our physical position and provide the feedback necessary for us to move and maintain our balance. For example, if you put your hands behind your back and wiggle your fingers, you know exactly where they are and how they are moving even though you can't see them. When you walk into a dark room in your house you can reach up to switch on the light accurately although you cannot see the switch or your hand. When the feedback system between proprioceptors and muscles is well developed through use, balance is constantly maintained (Crum, 1987).

How do the senses affect attention?

Parents and teachers often notice periods of physical awkwardness and lack of co-ordination in children who are in the midst of, or recently emerged from, growth spurts. What they are seeing is actually a lag between the body's growth and its proprioceptive sense of itself in space. When the proprioceptive sense adapts to the new sizes and proportions, the gawkiness disappears.

All the senses are processed low down in the brain (in the brain stem) before higher cortical functions like attention control and language and reasoning can occur.

The students have explained to them that, when they are sitting still and balanced in the listening position, they are using proprioception and the vestibular system to underpin the other senses like building blocks. **This makes the other senses work more effectively and therefore listening and looking are enhanced.** (See Building Blocks diagrams on p50.)

The students are taught to sit in the following **relaxed but alert** position:

- Bottoms to the rear of their chairs.
- Chairs tucked comfortably near to their desks.
- Feet planted firmly flat on the floor.
- Hands gently clasped together on the desk.
- Backs upright.

They are sitting with both feet firmly on the ground, the back is well supported and body is well balanced. They take in the teacher's message more clearly and therefore effective learning takes place.

Students who are slumped in their seats, leaning forward resting their head in their hands or lolling about in their chairs, will generally have a considerably reduced attention level because their proprioceptive and vestibular systems are distracting the brain into keeping their bodies upright.

Attention

When the proprioceptive system and the vestibular system are functioning well they support and enhance listening and looking i.e. attention.

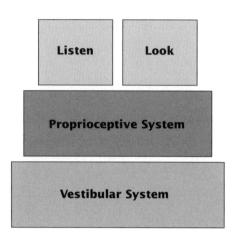

Disordered Attention

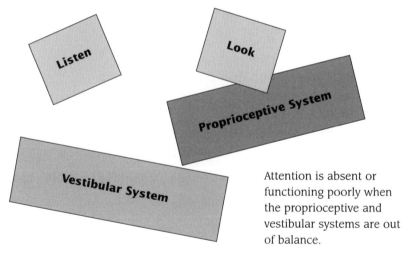

Attention is absent or functioning poorly when the proprioceptive and vestibular systems are out of balance.

Initially the students will complain that this listening position feels weird and uncomfortable. Many of them will seldom sit upright at home or at school. Anyone who has studied the Alexander Technique or yoga will know how strange it feels when learning to stand in a truly balanced position. Fairly quickly the students realise that they can maintain this listening position for several minutes at a time and that their bodies learn the posture in the same way they learn any new skill.

Session 2 Listening in the classroom

The purpose of this session is to:

- review active listening behaviours to aid long-term retention.

- identify behaviours that hinder learning for the individual and the whole class.

- identify why an individual might behave in that way.

- introduce the new sitting position and explain the physiological basis for this.

- practise the sitting position for listening.

- allow the students to experience the difference in learning when the whole class is completely focused.

Preparation

Trainers and teachers need to be familiar with the Learning Framework of Model – Analysis – Practice (see p47).

Classroom layout
All participants must be facing the teachers/trainers. Desks must be completely cleared.

Session Begins

Review
The adults remind the pupils that there are two sessions on listening skills: the first session covered listening to make friends, whilst this session will be about listening to learn. Both the posters, Listening to Make Friends and Listening to Learn can be displayed again. The adults ask the pupils to recall all the listening skills identified in the Session 1. These are written on the board and the pupils become competitive in striving to remember the fourteen skills they generated previously.

Homework

The pupils are reminded that they were asked to identify the listening behaviours of their families. Individuals are asked to share their observations with the class and how they felt when, for example, their brother ignored them. This often creates amusement and serves to reinforce the importance of good listening skills on the speaker.

Listening task – modelling poor listening

This is introduced as an opportunity to practise the listening skills just identified in the classroom. It is used in an amusing and surprising way to illustrate the ways pupils commonly disrupt teaching whether by accident or design. While one adult reads The Martian Space Wagon story the other sits amongst the pupils and continually disrupts them by a series of inappropriate actions.

Before they start Adult A explains to the class that he or she will read a description and they must listen carefully and then draw the item.

Adult B sits at a desk and disrupts Adult A throughout the reading, as described in the introduction on p47.

Analysis of the poor listening behaviours

Adult A asks, 'Could you listen and remember what to draw? Point to what was stopping you listening.' That is, of course Adult B.

The inappropriate behaviours are elicited and noted on the board.

The pupils are asked:

'How do you feel when someone behaves like that in class?'

Elicit the pupils' emotional response to such disruptive behaviour and how it stops their learning, for example, they feel angry, annoyed, frustrated.

The pupils are asked:

'Why do some people behave like that?'

Pupils usually have a keen understanding of the true motivation of such deliberate disrupters. Shape the responses towards: attention-seeking, unhappy, find learning difficult, wants admiration, may have difficulties at home.

Note the discrepancy between the need for approval and their peers true negative feelings towards them, that is, annoyed and frustrated.

Listening skills

Highlight the different skills needed for classroom versus social listening:

- Similar – eye contact, no fiddling, etc.

- Different – no nodding, no asking spontaneous questions, no small words.

The importance of a good sitting position

The pupils practise sitting by being asked to:

- Draw the chair into the desk comfortably.

- Sit with your bottom against the base of the chair-back so that your back is supported.

- Place both feet (and all chair-legs) on the floor to support the body.

- Rest arms on the desk, folded or on the lap, whichever is most comfortable. They should NOT be supporting the head, which leads to slumping.

The trainers emphasise the increase in attention when sitting in an upright and balanced posture. A poster is put up as a visual aid, saying Relaxed and Alert to remind pupils that: RELAXED ALERTNESS = the best posture for learning. The pupils are asked:

'What does alert mean?'

The teacher explains that as well as the five senses they already know they are using two other, very important senses – the proprioceptive and vestibular systems. The teacher can display the seven senses:

Sight	Sound	Smell	Taste
Touch	Proprioception	Vestibular System	

Acknowledge that this sitting position feels strange because they are not used to it. Play the following game **while they maintain the new sitting posture** to illustrate how quickly the brain learns to adapt to new positions as:

- Fold your arms.

- Note which hand/arm is uppermost.

- Fold your arms so that the other hand/arm is uppermost.

- Notice that this feels very strange to you.

- Repeat the changes a few times.

- The 'new' way quickly starts to feel more familiar because your brain is starting to form new connections, new pathways.

- This will happen with the new sitting posture when it is practised regularly.

This game can be repeated with interlocking the fingers of both hands together in your normal pattern and then interlocking them so the thumb and fingers of the opposite hand are uppermost.

N.B. The pupils will have maintained the new posture for around ten minutes by this time.

Practice of good listening skills

Ensure everyone is still sitting correctly and repeat the original listening task of The Martian Space Wagon with this increased level of attention and concentration.

(Adult B also listens well.) The teacher should be able to speak in a very quiet voice because the room is so still.

Highlight to the pupils how effective this simple change has been and how quickly they have learnt it. Ask pupils how it felt to listen that time to increase their awareness of the improvement.

Explain that this is their new posture for the first few minutes of the lesson to maximise their learning.

Explain to the students that there will be key phrases that the adults will use to remind them of their listening skills such as 'good sitting posture'.

Key phrases for attention and active listening

These can be used for:

- settling the class

- during initial instruction

  '**Good sitting posture**: this means feet flat on the floor, bring chair close in to your desk, put your bottom right back in the chair so you're sitting up straight, hands relaxed on the desk or on your lap.'

  '**Eye contact**: if you're looking at me I know you're listening.'

  '**No fidgeting or fiddling**: put pens or pencils down.'

  '**No interrupting or calling out**: hands up.'

These key phrases can be printed out and used as a poster, Key Phrases for Attention and Active Listening.

Pupils should complete their own posters for homework on What Helps Good Listening in Class and What Spoils Good Listening in Class. Ideally they should be able to discuss their homework during time with their form tutor and produce one final version for display in their tutor rooms, so that the skills can be constantly referred to.

Further activities can be used at the end of the session depending on the time available.

Resources for Session 2 – Classroom Listening

A selection of games and worksheets are included for reinforcement of the students' listening skills.

Materials

- Relaxed and Alert Poster
- The Martian Space Wagon sheet
- What Helps Good Listening in Class
- What Spoils Listening in Class
- Key Phrases for Attention and Active Listening

Games

Eye contact with the teacher

The rules of the game are explained.

- The teacher talks to the class about any topic.
- When the teacher blinks several times the students stand up.
- When the teacher closes his/her eyes the students put their arms in the air.

Comment on the eye contact observed and its importance in attention.

When the class are successful with this game, the teacher may like to extend it into lesson time.

Listening to the teacher

Noises off

The teacher warns the students that they may hear some strange things today and to indicate if they hear one by putting up their hand.

A concealed squeaky toy could be sounded a few minutes into the lesson.

Comment on the listening skills observed.

Farmyard

The teacher explains that the students must listen carefully for some animal names that will crop up as the day progresses. It is best to prepare this because it is not easy to do spontaneously. It is easiest to do this with any notices that are to be given out.

The lesson begins and the teacher slips animal words into his/her sentences, for example:

'After lunch today we will dog go out into the hall.'

'We are looking sheep at some books...'

Comment on the listening skills observed.

Story game

- Divide the class into groups e.g. bicycles, cars and lorries.

- Tell them a story about a child's journey to visit the zoo.

- As the teacher mentions an item of transport the group has to wave their hands or stand up depending on the level of physical interaction the group needs.

Comment on the listening skills observed.

The Martian Space Wagon

The Space Wagon is like a people carrier. It has a long body, with a round front and a flat back. The body is made of shiny, shimmering tiles that look like the scales on a fish. The front is round like a glass bowl. The drivers have a good view all round them. There is no door into the Space Wagon, but there is a hatch on top with an aerial poking out. There is a hoist to lift the driver up to the hatch. The Space Wagon has no wheels but it glides along on a huge black rubbery cushion. There is a name painted on the Space Wagon – 'Boodles' – and a blue and white flag flies from the aerial.

Relaxed and Alert

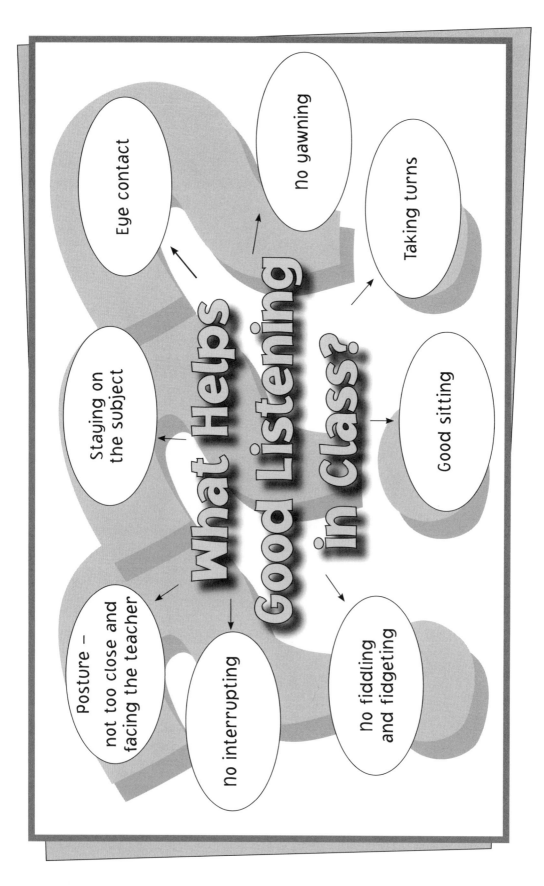

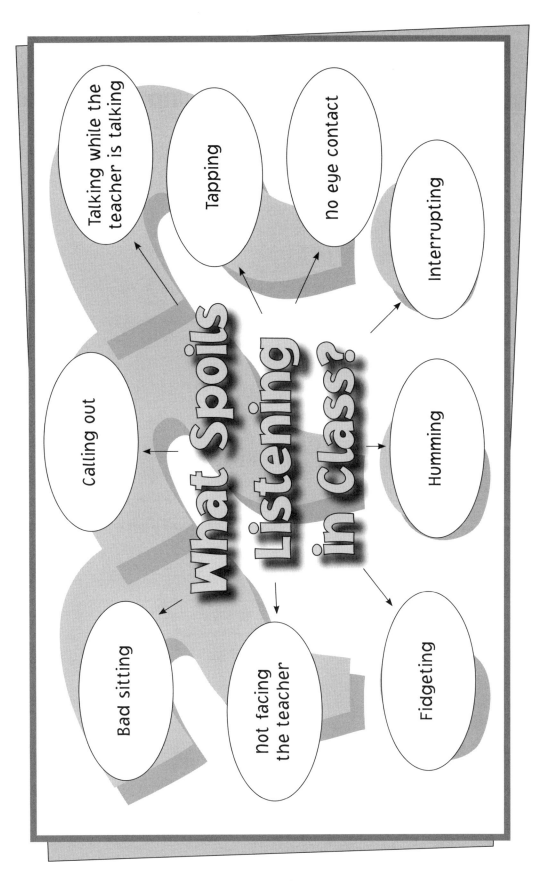

Key Phrases for Attention and Active Listening

Good sitting posture

- Feet flat on the floor.
- Bottom right back in the chair so you're sitting up straight.
- Hands relaxed on the desk or on your lap.

Eye contact

- If you're looking at me I know you're listening.

No fidgeting or fiddling

- Fidgeting (with pens, bags, hair, tapping, humming) distracts the rest of us and we can't learn.

No interrupting

- We all take turns.
- If you interrupt you must think you are more important than the person speaking.
- No calling out.
- No talking when the teacher is talking.

Follow-up Work

In order to review and maintain active listening behaviours it is necessary to remind the students of what those behaviours are, at a suitable interval after the two training sessions.

The success of any programme relies upon it being practised and used frequently to effect consolidation. This programme is no different. It is really successful when the learners are regularly reminded of the skills they have learnt, to maximise their auditory attention at every opportunity.

During the maintenance period and before the booster session, every teacher needs to remind the pupils to adopt the listening position and use the key phrases, such as 'Good sitting posture'. The individual skills need to be named rather than referred to in general terms. For example, when a student interrupts or fidgets during teacher instruction times, rather than saying, 'Remember your listening skills', poor listening behaviours should be identified by asking:

'What is that behaviour called?'

By asking the student to identify the behaviour, it helps him/her to become aware of what he/she is doing when it happens and to remedy it.

Students have been asked to make up their own posters on 'What Helps Good Listening in Class?' and 'What Spoils Listening in Class?' (copies included in this publication) and these should be displayed in every classroom. They can also be stuck in their daily organisers to take with them as reminders.

Session 3

Booster Session

Booster Session

Six to eight weeks after Session 2, the two adults involved in the first two sessions carry out a 10–20 minute booster session to give the students another practice in the sitting position and to review all the skills required.

Checklist for Booster Session

The adults ask all pupils to adopt the good listening position and carefully check that each individual demonstrates all aspects of this position.

The class is asked to remember all 14 listening skills and these are written up.

Pupils may identify and comment upon any change they have noted in themselves or others in their:

- listening
- learning
- general behaviour
- learning environment.

This discussion provides a very valuable opportunity for the students to reflect upon the progress that they have made in the interim that they may not have been conscious of. It will help them to encourage and support one another.

Students can state whether they have achieved the target skill they set themselves and also whether they need to set a new target for themselves.

Students should also complete the Review Questionnaire so that an overall picture can be gained. This questionnaire will identify how useful the students are finding the skills, how often they are reminded to use them and where they use them most. The results of the questionnaire will also identify gaps in general practice.

Review Questionnaire

To be completed six to eight weeks after the programme has been finished.

Name _____ Date _____

How has my listening improved?

How has my learning improved?

How has the general behaviour of the whole class improved?

My target
listening skill was _____

My new target
listening skill is _____

Please mark on the grid below

How well you used to listen

0   1   2   3   4   5   6   7   8   9   10

How well you listen now

0   1   2   3   4   5   6   7   8   9   10

Poor   Excellent

Bibliography

Basic Skills Agency (2003) *Young Children's Skills on Entry to Education.*

Christakis, D., Dimitri, A., Zimmerman, F.J., DiGiuseppe & D.L., McCarty, C.A. (2004) Early television exposure and subsequent attentional problems in children. *Journal of Paediatrics*, Vol. 113.

Crum, Thomas F., (1987) *The Magic of Conflict: Turning A Life into A Work of Art.* New York: Simon & Schuster.

DfEE, 2001. *Key Stage 3 National Strategy Framework for Teaching English.*

Galton, M., Hargreaves, L., Comber, C., Wall, D. & Pell, A. (1999) *Inside the Primary Classroom; 20 years on.* London, Routledge & Keegan Paul.

Hart, B. & Risley, T. (1995) *Meaningful Differences in the Everyday Experience of Young American Children.* Baltimore: Paul H. Brookes Publishing Company Inc.

Hastings, Nigel, Chantry Wood, Karen (2000) Spacing for Learning in Primary Classrooms: Bridging the Gaps. Paper presented at the British Educational Research Association Conference.

Healey, Jane. (1991) *Endangered Minds: Why Our Children Don't Think and What To Do About It.* New York: Simon and Schuster.

Hernandez-Peon, R. (1969) *Neurophysiology of Attention.* In P.J. Vinkin & G.W. Bruyn (eds.), *Handbook of Clinical Neurology.* Amsterdam: North Holland Pub.

Karrass, J., Braungart-Rieker, J., Mullins, J., & Burke Lefever, J. (2002) Processes in language acquisition: the roles of gender, attention, and maternal encouragement of attention over time. *Journal of Child Language*, Vol. 29.

Locke, A., Ginsborg, J. & Peers, I. Development and disadvantage: implications for the early years and beyond (2002). *International Journal of Language & Communication Disorders*, 1 January, Vol. 37, no. 1, pp. 3-15(13).

Plowden Report (1967) *Children and their Primary Schools.* HMSO.

Tomatis, Alfred A. (1991). *The Conscious Ear, My Life of Transformation through Listening.* Barrytown, New York: Station Hill Press.

Tortora, Gerard J. & Nicholas P., Anagnostakos (1990) *Principles of Anatomy and Physiology.* Sixth Edition. New York: Harper.

Ward, S. (1984) Detecting abnormal behaviours in infancy: the relationship between such disorders and linguistic development. *British Journal of Disorders of Communication*, 17, 35-42.

Empathy

Promoting Resilience and Emotional Intelligence for Students Aged 7 to 10 Years

Bob Bellhouse *Teacher, researcher, writer and publisher*, **Andrew Fuller** *Clinical Psychologist, Victoria, Australia* and **Glenda Johnston** *Educational Psychologist, Victoria, Australia*

Empathy is a fundamental building block for the positive development and mental health of children. It is central to the development of conscience, love, friendship and kindness. This programme supports the encouragement and teaching of empathy and resilience and schools will reap the benefits in their students' achievements.

Identifying key elements that help young people to develop empathic feelings and behaviour, it helps schools to:

- create structures that promote connectedness and belonging
- provide learning experiences that build excitement about learning and hopefulness and possibility for their futures

Activities include 'The Circle of Friendship', which builds empathy into the day-to-day operation of the classroom in a highly motivating and visual way. All 10 sessions include teacher notes, experiential activities, worksheets, games and reflective questions that will encourage young people to explore the different elements of empathic behaviour. Many more ideas for developmental work are also included.

June 2005 · 64 pages
Paperback & CD-ROM (1-4129-1159-1)

On the Same Side

133 Stories to Help Resolve Conflict

Francisco Ingouville *International Mediator, Buenos Aires*

This captivating resource is for anyone who is interested in learning more about using negotiation and mediation to settle conflicts positively and effectively. Francisco's engaging and amusing book of memories, anecdotes and examples draws on his own experience to illustrate the vast array of human conflict and solutions.

The stories can be used to:
- generate discussion
- stimulate thinking in assemblies
- enrich mediation training
- support win//win positions
- help those in conflict find solutions.

You will find many different meanings and complex ideas embedded in these insightful, light-hearted and fascinating narratives. This is a book that you'll come back to time after time.

April 2005 · 136 pages
Paperback (1-4129-1079-X)

For more details and to order, visit
www.paulchapmanpublishing.co.uk

P·C·P
Paul Chapman
Publishing

Outside the Circle

A Video Story with Activities to Combat Racism and Prejudice for Young People Aged 7 to 11

Simon Firth *Writer and Actor, London*

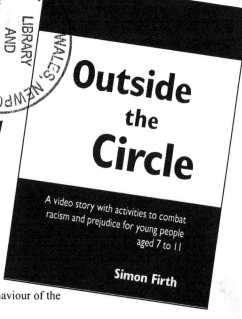

Outside the Circle tells the story of child who experiences name-calling and teasing because he is considered by his peers to be 'different'. He experiences sensations of confusion, anger, isolation and low self esteem, before his teacher intervenes to help him, and change the behaviour of the other children.

By taking the audience on this emotional journey, it is hoped to increase empathetic understanding of how it feels to be made fun of and teased and called names. Crucially children are encouraged to understand that all name calling is wrong, and that we all are different and have the right to be respected for what we are.

The story should be open to interpretation as a story about 'difference' and 'bullying'. It need not be understood as a story about racism for younger children. However, children, particularly children in predominantly white schools, will encounter racism, and the project is intended to enable you to open consideration of anti-racism within your school.

The project will provide a starting point for work on anti-racism in schools. This video is a recording of a live performance in which Simon illustrates the pain and desperation experienced by a child who is excluded by his peers and suffers racist name-'' ' rejection.

Simon's follow-up notes and activities suggest ways in which the video incorporated into the citizen curriculum and help schools to tackle this importa. difficult aspect of school and community life.

Contents: Simon Firth - His Work \ Project Objectives \ Methodology \ Reporting an Recording Racist Incidents \ Teaching Anti-racism in Predominantly White Schools Engaging Children in the Formulation of School Policy \ Before Watching Outside the Circle \ Teacher Notes: Unit One - What is Racism? Unit Two - What Do We Know About Racism? Unit Three - Research Findings Unit Four - Conclusion and Drafting a Student Statement of Policy Follow-up Lesson Ideas - Ages 5 to 7 Follow-up Lesson Ideas - Ages 8 to 11 \ Activities to Use After Watching the Video \ About Gripping Yarns \ Pupil Evaluation - Outside the Circle \ Playground Picture \ Bibliography

June 2005 · 40 pages
Video and booklet (1-4129-1070-6)

For more details and to order, visit
www.paulchapmanpublishing.co.uk

P·C·P
Paul Chapman
Publishing